Love
where the nights are green

Rienzi Crusz

© Rienzi Crusz 2007

Cover Painting   **Richard Gabriel**
Cover Design   **Michael Crusz**
Layout Design   **Sudath Attanayake/Tulana Media Unit, Sri Lanka**

Printed at Pandora Press
Kitchener, Ontario

Published by Pasdeloup Press
Stratford, Ontario

ISBN 0-920214-11-8
Published in a limited edition.

For Anne,
so close to the ways of flowers

This is all there is and this is everything

- Joyce Carol Oates

ACKNOWLEDGEMENTS

Some of these poems first appeared in the
following journals:

The Malahat Review, The Antigonish Review,
Prairie Schooner, Grail, Canadian Forum, Quarry,
Fiddlehead, The Toronto Review, The New
Quarterly, The University of Windsor Review,
Ariel, The Globe and Mail, Possibilities, Prism
International, Descant.

CONTENTS

1

LEGACY   FOR ANNE

Take my poems ----
I have nothing else of value to give you.
Fruits
of lonely nights, faithful candles
that flamed and sputtered until
my metaphors were right.

Take my poems ----
my kingdom of fears in harness,
days of silence
when my neighbouring world
danced its tumultuous jig
and laughed.

Take my poems ----
they were born with a brown skin,
sang with a brown voice,
danced a brown jig, persevered,
until the cold white paper
took in my words with the music
and fatted calf of the prodigal story.

Take my poems ----
my umber heart   my umber words,
the forgotten pain, the remembered music,
the new landscape,
why I thought God was a poem,
the poem, the only cosmic poet.

Take my poems ----
mostly, because I love you,
they are the bloodstones
of my youth, fading footsteps of age,
small bouquets
that may, perhaps, survive a little while
like a memory.

Nothing else comes to mind,
the house is only wood and cabook,
the money is paper.

HOW DOES ONE REACH THE SWEET KER-NEL?

The way
the Ceylonese farmer
husks the coconut:
a crowbar planted in the ground,
and the iron tooth jabs the skin;

the flesh tears
till the bone shows round and clean;
the hammer of machete
on the skull,
the milk leaks
and the sweet kernel opens out
like a womb.

For the kind of love
that hangs exotic and hard
like a bunch of king-coconuts
on the palm of our dreams,
we need to tear the pink fibres
on our crowbar nerves,
machete the shell of stubborn eyes
and burst into the kernel
of the heart.

Gentility,
that warm tentative hand,
will only do
in the kind of love that shares
the breed of plums.

THE COMPANIONS

A house-fly
    with one silken wing
sat on the crest
    of my eyelash,
gazed into my moon-blue eyes
    and turned green.
I heard a swish of wing,
    an echo
of falling bone.

A mosquito,
    the same that thundered
in my ears last night,
    shuffled its shadowy feet
on the nape of my neck,
    curtsied
and plunged a needle
    into my pink skin.

I heard a collapse of bone,
    saw the floor open its dusty mouth
like a spider's trap .

A lady, lovely,
    with gypsy bangles singing
from her enamel wrists
    touched my shoulder,
the blood surged into my skull,
    and the carpet gently collected me
into its nylon arms.

WHAT IF

What if
the ticking night beetle
that chose silence
to gnaw the guava's heart,
was no beetle at all.

What if
the midnight bat
with the red mouth of a woman
drank the thick syrup
of the cadju-pulang,
and was no bat at all.

What if
the sweet red jambu
sensuous with new rain,
turning white and vinegar
at the biting,
was no jambu at all.

What if
the incandescent moth
that scattered its pin bones
to the flame,
was no moth at all.

In the beginning,
Eden
was the pink heart of the guava,
the pulang the honey-bee's hive,
jambu, the color of July,
and the delicate moth
fashioning dance out of flame,
burning and not burning.

THE GARDENER

Since Adam
had fouled things up
by trying to live under God
with a naked woman, a serpent,
and an apple tree,
this gardener's ambition
was to remake Eden
in only a garden of roses.

He would tell the story
of his labours
through lean dark years
in the grief of scars
on his thick knuckles,
his calloused palms
where dirt had churned
the beginnings of flowers.

When God's hot breath
finally broke rain,
and roses exploded
under his disciplined eyes,
he still couldn't claim
the Eden before the apple,

for one wild sunflower rose,
seeded unknown
in his boundaries of perfection,
cheating his guillotine of weeds,
reared her saffron head
and cried: pick me,
and I'll sing you a song
of first love.

As the sunflower petals
teased through his fingers,
each falling
like small symmetrical suns
at his feet,   echoes
of childhood games:
I love you, I love you not,
I love you, I love you not.

The rim of soft fire
now almost undone,
the last petal throbbing
like a dark exotic woman
in his arms, softly breathing:

I am Eden, before, after, and now.

ELEGY FOR AN ORANGE

How your roundness
throbs to titillate,
dress of furious saffron
takes my eyes;
and your skin, soft as diaper,
a snow-flake to the touch,
floods my island of nerves,
collects water in my mouth.

But I cannot love you,
cannot seduce you;
I want you in totality,
a chemistry of assimilation.
You have to die,
tortured for your exotic perfections:
my thumb in your throat,
one heave, and I burst you open.
Blood spills.
I taste you limb by limb,
wanting you only
in the tongue's orgasm
of your sun-ripe death.

SOLITUDE

Solitude I love you,
I believe in you, do not betray me
(Ernesto Sanchez)

This rare moment,
naked to myself, the spinning world,
this deadly brew (of pure freedom)
that moulds my moods to heaven and hell,
gives mouth to God, stone and tree,
the lamp-post woman, the child
with teddy bear in its arms.

This rare moment
when you are mine,
 scream from the belly, the hairy head,
show me your madness of laughter,
the blood on your hands;
let the monsoon thunder roll in,
the beauty and vulgarity of words.

Give me, again and again
these rare moments
with which to play the extravagant moods
of men, the farrago world
like a new symphony,
with no man, no world,
ever knowing , ever listening.

THE INTERVIEW

Two TV cameras trained like guns,
    I, the Sun-Man,
your caressing eyes,
    and the count down...

You coax me into beginnings,
    past inventions in the snow,
then deftly persuade deeper fires,
    my thin Canadian ice
to thaw in my throat,
    the maple leaf smudge in my passport.

I am in the mouth of the sun,
    the Immigrant Song;
how I hear the elephant in my sleep;
    white landscape in ruins,
I find my own green forest, island sea;
    the ocelot's eye, the jambu bleeds,
my childhood
    in the claws of the sand-crab.

And what shaped your book
    Flesh and Thorn ?
Blood on the sun,
    the Scarlet Ibis blurred in the swamp,
deceit crouched in the crotch,
    'love with his gift of pain'.

Suddenly, I split the act in two,
    juggle two red balls,
the poem made, the poem becoming:
    I swim in your saucer eyes,
fingers search the curved fruit
    under your shirt,
I nose ebony configurations,
    dream the almond under the husk...

THE WEDDING PHOTO
AND THE GECKOES OF
EVENING

Under pale fluorescent light
   the happy couple
   still poses sepiatone
   for memory, future generations,
   though best-man and bridesmaid
   now wear the blur of mould,
   look casual as footnotes.

As if to a framed magnet
   they crawl
   from their dark cobwebbed corners,
   geckoes of the evening, prophets
   that suck the white-washed walls and wait
   for the moths to play
   their daily ritual of death.

One shrill cry, then another
   and another...
   The whole household listens
   to the dark decibels of prophecy,
   and writes out the diagrams
   of their own shadowed lives.

Look how this one crawls
   the length of his body,
   parades its glass stomach black
   with insect bones,
   how the pale head juts,
   the minute eyeballs swivel
   over the wedding's blur
   and come up with nothing.

The handsome couple
  are said to have lived
  happily ever after.
  So, my soothsayers of the twilight hour,
  the white-washed wall,
  what is your verdict ?

Why, I never heard a sound
  escape your lightning tongues,
  as if there were no legends to sing,
  no prophecies to make, no wings
  to dare the fluorescent flame.

Had you, for once,
  found truth
  in the scarred runnels of the dumb throat,
  the deep shadows of silence?

PARDON MY MUTED WAYS
(FOR WENDY)

This midnight absence of fire,
and your eyes asking the silent questions:

Why a Christ
on every hair of your head,
metaphors delicate as wind,
those frightened gestures
from some past prophecy of pain?

From you
who once set fire to wet grass
with torches in your limbs,
coaxed suns like butterflies
on to your open palms,
spoke words as passionate
as elephants trumpeting the moon?

Pardon my muted ways,
lovely Jewish girl,
the monsoon surf should have pounded
on your white belly reef,
the sun grown vermilion
from the exotic spread of the peacock.

But once long ago,
a haunting face
drained the Sun-Man to pale bone,
till night collapsed his eyes
and love slept off its wounds.

Tomorrow,
a cloud-burst of blue rain,
the sun-fish turning their green mouths
to the erotic eye of the moon,

bougainvillea bulbing
with the orgasm of a new sun.

A TOUCH OF FEVER

She came
all young and curved
to the Library Reference Desk
and asked for information
on Simon and Garfunkel
and I gave her
a sheaf of crow hair
two walnut eyes
and the music
of a soul   burnt
to pink ash

WITH THE TEMPESTUOUS MYTHS OF BIRDS

(FOR WENDY)

As St. Agatha's old pub
holds its children
in the warm glow
of beer laughter,
she's making the poem:

with mannerisms
of glass bangles on her wrists,
lips that brand
the opening lines,
a mood for the thoughts of evening men.

She packs meat
into the poem's body
with shoulders that ripple
like stalking lioness,
her breasts held firm
and flowing
in the discipline of the spring.

A cat uncurls,
silently feeds
on my hot thoughts, taps
the blood-beat under my skin.
A warm bird is eating
from her hands.

She reveals appetite,
the way she flings those eyes,
turns her head
to catch the fire of chandeliers,
and yet builds distance
with sudden deep silences.

Thoughts, perhaps,
of hunter turning hunted,
a sense of eagle
violating sun,
swooping majestically for twigs
to build a nest between her thighs.

But she's now
beyond touching,
the poem's snare knotted
in tight perfection.

As St.Agatha's children
all unravel into the cold street,
the poet   alone   sleeps
with the tempestuous myths of birds.

MOODS

How like the lotus
you silently unhinge
your silken limbs,
spread your head
on the mud-brown carpet
and wait
for the Bird of Paradise
to graze its wings
about your exotic thighs.

I sing
as the warm sea flutters
and swirls round my brown skin;
the Talapath and Seer
heady with the red sun on their fins,
and thorned coral altars blazing
a flame of seaweed
about my fierce nobility.

FOR THE UNFAITHFUL ONE

You walk
into this room
and the stallion shadow
on the wall
hardens to a lump;

you part
your exotic lips
to spill the ache of truth,
and the moth
under the veranda light
tumbles in flame.

How you once
walked naked
in the embracing sun,
and the oriole
stole the fire
of your breasts,
the sun-flower
held its breath,

and I was there
to gather in your loveliness
like an adolescent lover.

JUST LIKE THAT

First, the dream: glaciers.
   One in particular.
Stunning radiance on its Arctic face
   as it's caught
in the lasso of the sun.

Suddenly, it lets out
   a cracking rumble, then walks;
boulder hips,
   white gargantuan buttock and thighs,
cleave the seas
   like some mountain prow.
A lone gull hovers,
   smells the promise of death,
and wheels away.
   Just like that.

Then morning.
   The last Act, without first or second.
Not a word or gesture,
   cheerio, goodbye or chiao,
and you turn on your wornout heels
   and walk into the falling snow.
Just like that.

How do I read your Alzheimer going ?
   Remember the matslide   the swings
in the back yard,
   those caring hands that swung the hammer
for the tree-house on the old Maple,
   the magnum opus of your summer days,
your brick barbecue ?

So what if the water-softener hungers
    for its forty pounds of salt,
the heavy lounge needs moving
    from the bay-window sun?
There's sherry and roses on the coffee table,
    Roger Williams on the keys;
you crook my tired bones in your gentle arms,
    pluck the rose between my thighs;
your baby daughter is dreaming
    in the cradle of your eyes,

and you, of a sudden,
    with stones in your mouth,
turn on your wornout heels
    and walk out into the showering snow.

Just like that.

KARMA

The going away in June
was cruel. I saw the gull
flee the salty spray
and linger on wet rock
with the fading smell
of frangipani.

How purple grape
crushed in the black hands
havocked in the heart.
The empty space shaped
to the slim body mocking
the bleeding eyes,
the nerves stretched along
the fluid horizon,

the eyes turned,
the mind shifted,
and the hills stirred
to the valley deeps,
and the healing sun
sealed the hemophiliac flow.

How the valley bloomed
to new poems
written on olive skins,
the empty space to giant pizzas
from Ponzanelli's,
the thirsty rock to cocktails
brewed and shaken
to Valentino's recipe.
How the smell of frangipani

gently surrendered
to the magic of lotions
and brandy on the rocks.

How the small linear star
melted to the fluid circle
of the sun,
and her gilded voice leaped
from the cougar's throat,
the moon spilled
her lotus eyes
and white rock sprouted
with raven hair.
How the blue water at Fergus Dam
thrashed the soft brown skin,
the sun face.

A slim Singhala girl
stretched in his bones
across the wide open world,

the vine hangs heavy again
with purple grape.

TASTE OF OLD WINE

After ten years
on replay
in slow motion
the way
she killed me off

seemed clean
and surgical
a poem
spilling
from the tongue
of the jewelled cobra

The spring moment
when I searched
her eyes, jumped
the cool mercury
to summer pitch

she slowly turned
her polished head
caught me
in pale blue gun-sights
and gently squeezed
the trigger

At the time
it was sound
and lightning pain
of whiplash
blue shrapnel
demanding silence
All along
she knew
the ways of flowers.

THE NIGHT BEFORE MY BIRTHDAY

The dream
went something like this:
in a naked house, white,
 breathing the smell of DETTOL,
like an empty ward
with its mouth open
for the coming of the lame and the limp.

My Spanish furniture,
pictures , poetry books, all gone;
the flight
        of velvet drapes,
        warm dust of trivia,
        many years of matured griefs,
        red joys that burned in dark corners,
and the smell of children
                        scraped out
by some detergent hand.

My ex-wife crawls,
a fluid limbo-dancer,
from under the slit of door:
all rags, her face caked like a ghost,
she asks: Where are the children?
Fled, fled, I cry.
Noah's doves seek the olive branch.
And the gods of Kataragama
bleed in their shrines
as a whiff of frangipani
cuts through the antiseptic air
and disappears.

And I am born
into another year
with the taunt of warm fires
burnt out,
faces of children   lost
in the jungle of new apartments,
old scars
    hurting like wounds,
    the raging chaos of love.

2

ROOTS
(FOR CLETA NORA MARCELLINA SERPANCHY)

What the end usually demands
is something of the beginning,
and so
I conjure history from a cup
of warm Portuguese blood
from my forefathers,
black diamond eyes, charcoal hair
from my Sinhalese mothers;
the beached catamaran,
gravel voices of the fishermen,
the catch still beating like a heart
under the pelting sun;
how the pariah dogs looked urgent
with fish-meal in their brains,
the children romped, sagged,
then melted into the sand.

A Portuguese captain holds
the soft brown hand of my Sinhala mother.
It's the year 1515 A.D.,
when two civilizations kissed and merged,
and I, burgher of that hot embrace,
write a poem of history
as if it were only the romance
of a lonely soldier on a crowded beach
in Southern Ceylon.

ELEGY FOR THE SUN-MAN'S FATHER

Father,
you were a great mathematician,
loved God and the jambu fruit.

How can I, a child,
trace even a tangent
to your perfect geometries,
the vast afternoons of your brain
in which you walked so easily
with Euclid and Pythagoras?

And how can I compose
that mathematical prayer
of your living, the way
you chased the ultimate equation,
the something that flowed
from heaven to earth,
earth to heaven?

I know. I'll use my crayons
to draw a perfect tangent
straight to the tip of your tongue:
Ah, the fruit of jambu!
How I shuddered and shook the tree,
and you and I
shared the sweet pulp
of our mouth's yearnings.

ELEGY #2   (for Dad)

Morning. Black hammering of crow
trying to tell me something?

Sudden magpie   alone
promising sorrow to wear on my face.

That same night, I heard the jak-tree owl hoot
from its darkened throat.

Cats took the parapet wall and caterwauled
their psalms for the dying.

Father, you died with morning on your face,
fulfilling the prophecies of birds.

I, rocked in the hammock of the sun,
your gentle ways,

refused the dark harbingers,
saw nothing

in the sliced face of the moon,
the broken reservoirs of your heart,

only believed   the God
on your wizened face,

your love   now silent
and hard as wood.

MARGINS

Into the first minute
of my math lesson with my father,
and he raps my knuckles, foot-ruler
resonating like a tuning fork.

"Margins, stupid, margins,
no math without margins!" he shouts.
"Think of chaos --
a world without order,
 safety nets, margins
for human error ".

Tears. No argument.
Not against a man who, I was told,
argues with Euclid and Pythagoras in his dreams.
Mother's vain protests
from the far corners of her kingdom:
"Dear, I asked you to teach the child,
not hit him!"

Margins — the discipline, the magic,
and I'm ready
for life's cruel tracasserie.
Hold the surging blood, swear words,
duck into shoulder lanes, corridors,
let the insurgent moments pass:

this neighbour who, every spring,
unravels somebody's dog-shit
on his front lawn, bares
his yellow teeth & glares
over the privet hedge;

this flock of mad starlings,
raucous spill from their dark throats,
the karma of a lone sparrow
with stone-shot eyes
hurtling to its untimely death;

this exotic woman
who lures me to her thatched lair, dark
but for a thin shaft of moonlight,
then disappears into the shadows
of the sleeping coconut trees;

this sky that corrals its drifting clouds,
unloads its cold burden and laughs,
and down here all laughter's fled,
the song-bird's gone, nowhere
on the apple tree.

Margins: a father's love
for the systematic, spatial havens,
his kind of exercise book,
where the mathematical numbers could dance
well within the footlights;

his profound metaphor
for survival— safety exits, corridors,
a kind of narrow benevolence,
where the beserk moods of the mind,
the crashing moments are bypassed
without a whimper.

FOR CLETA NORA MARCELLINA SER-
PANCHY

Dead and not dead.
Gone and here,
you serve breakfast as usual:
hoppers and chicken curry,
coconut *sambol*, tea in the old pot
Talking as you serve, questioning
as you move around the table:
have you brushed your teeth, child?
Washed your face? Done your homework?

Yes, yes, the answers mumble,
hoppers greater than truth,
half-done sums
no match for chicken curry or coconut *sambol*.

Yes, I grieve no more, grieve truly.
For grief is nothing without memory,
as love is nothing without the proven deed.
Night comes quickly by.
Your small hands lay out the straw mats,
three for your brood of eight;
nor do you forget the ritual
of hot milk and Ovaltine for nightcap,
and we close our restless day
with tongues on our saucers like hungry cats.

And how you shaped
 the plum promise of Christmas:
Chinese crackers, bundles and bundles of them
tucked carefully in the *almirah's* bosom;
smell of French polish,
you on your knees squeezing out the shine
from veranda chairs, red cement floors,
a mirror to your sweating face;
and what about the milk-wine bottles
preaching their own sweet vapours?

I gaze once more at that one photograph
with the deep scowl on your face.
You believing truly that rod and child
went together, love held deep
in your small fists. And your cure
for my brother Hilary's greed for soda pop?
Immersion theory: a case of pop, one rattan cane,
your hectoring presence,
until he could drink no more,
was duly exorcised.

And me, your immigrant child of the snows?
How in once foolish times
when all hope was gone
and the Afghan moneylender
loomed like a shadow of death
on my threshold,
you threw in the deeds to your house,
your money, your gentle voice of caution:
"Take care, child, take care."

All this
and how you loved the rose ---
with cow-dung, bonemeal and crushed egg-shells;
the pomegranate tree
always so heavy with promise,
the shoe-flower hedge pruned to a prayer.

Mother, you are dead and not dead.
Gone and here: love, as the pappadams
crackle on your skillet again,
and you are shouting and chiding,
raving and ranting   loving,
praying, always praying.

ELEGY FOR THE SUN-MAN'S CHILDREN GOING

FOR DAPHNE, JOHN AND MARIA

How he plunged bravely
from sun to snow,
made perfect metaphor
from elephant and ice,
the breath of his sun children,
but never stepped out of the womb.

Time ran his fingers
thro their spring-rained hair,
saw their small bodies burgeon
like new grass, fashion words
from the puberty of a season;

and June broke cottage carnival,
their sun
spun headily on a frisbee,
love on the shuttlecock's nose,
the barbecue ripening like summer fruit;

and he shared their days
of shedding leaves,
winter's cruel gaucherie,
a stylish log-fire
in his rice, and curry and heart.

But the road that forked
like a divided vein,
took in its restless travellers,
and Daphne was gone, Maria is going,
and John contemplates the cobalt sky
with adolescent eyes, the possible mileage
in his dirty sneakers.

This immigrant poet,
whose road was never his , but went,
taking them to the junction
of their dreams, a pilgrim
without pilgrimage, his altar
still like the warm smooth stone
that stayed in the sun.

LOVE POEM FOR ANNE

For you , brown lover,
with buffalo curd and palmyrah honey
still sweet on your lips,
the raven winging in your hair,

I offer the immigrant land
with no contrary season,
only summer,
and summer and summer.

No white laming cold before the thaw,
no cutting nodule of spring,
no fallen leaves to confuse your feet,
only the consummate thing,

the full-blown rose, the sun
in batik exuberance.

Now also ask for the sweet warm rain,
the once harvest of fruit:
jambu, mango and mangosteen;
guava and rambuttan, the tender cadju

wrapped in green leaves, the jaggery bell
of the godambara-rotti man,
and I will tease the Asian condiment
from the summer almirahs of this land.

What you deserve will be
what you always had
in your warm rich blood:
the green land.

SANDWICH MAKER

What happens
when the lunch bag
breathes tuna, tuna, tuna,
Monday through Friday?
have bulls gone the way
of the dinosaur, pigs
taken wing
and melted into the trees?

I gaze at the Food Machine,
catch labels
on its revolving mouths:
Ham and Cheese, Pastrami on Rye,
Roast Beef...
Which makes me dream
of Zehr's fat butcher,
Angelo's Deli up the street.

So why has the loving wife
fallen hopelessly
into this fishy mode,
lazy repitition,
this enormity
that comes so easily
with tuna and mayonnaise
on five days a week?

I hear explanations
loud and smarting as whips:
fish cuts the cholesterol,
keeps down the weight,
controls your pressure.
I don't hear dark words
like boring, bland,
and by week's end, disgusting .

So this is the time
to let loose the demons,
give words the voice of imps,
write the poem
that I always wanted to,
invent a jungle
against my quiet despair
and listen
to the explosion
in the boring heart of the tuna sandwich.

AT THE WEDDING OF THE LAKE

Just when I thought
this was the real dream:
   doing nothing.
A stone sleeps in Twin Willows,
Simcoe salt under the skin
and every rib grins in silence
at other people
slowly beating themselves to death
from nine to five.

A seducing sun
pries open an eyelid:
Elmhurst Beach
holds its cottage children
 like plums in its soft hand:
Daphne, batik bikini on bronze,
lies surrendered,
and old Mr McIver, safely sun-glassed,
bares his rumpled chest
and savours the popsicle of the sun.

There's Maria
               sun-dancing,
whipping foam
from the Lake's shallow mouth
with tiny sticks of arms and legs;
John curls his coffee bones
to build my castles on the sand.

A blue boat springs,
divides the green seersucker skin,
froths at the prow
and wheels away towards the horizon.
And I, an old poet,
sit on this pier, a witness
to the red rabbi of sun
finally chanting the wedding psalm
for Simcoe Lake and Simcoe sky,
as a lone gull locks its wings
and glides in the amen of an arc.

THE SUN-MAN ENCOUNTERS ANNE LANDERS

He lost most of his mik teeth
while playing in the woods.
Under the silent shade
of na and jak
he could hear his bicuspids grow.

At five,
he watched two paddy-birds
wrap the red sun
under their wings
and copulate in the grass.

At ten,
he would giggle no more
at mongrels
growing the seeds of puppies
on the stone fires
of Colombo's streets.

At twenty-five,
he married
and had three children.
He now understood better
why a leopard one night
wounded a blue moon
when it didn't hear
an answering call
through the listening trees;
and the tremble of trumpets
was also the elephant
spilling the hot libido
of the jungle.

At forty-five,
he paces and shakes
the snow hours one evening
as the adrenalin leaked:
how he would like
to crush his glass of Arrack
with bare hands,
lap the red flow
with the tongue of cats
and refuse to believe
that a long-haired creature
was holding his daughter's hand
on her first date.

When Ann Landers
walks out of her column
with a bucket
full of quenching words:
Cool it, baby,
the sun is fixed
but the moon shows many faces,
the night, the silhouettes of dreams;

let the spring flow
through tall grass and fern,
gambol over green stones,
spill and froth over the gorge,
plunge into blue rivers
till it reaches
the bosom of the sea.

Soon you'll gaze at a red boat
                              lolling
on the waters,
with a happy fisherman
reeling in his catch.

MY SON

My son,
the blood I spilled for you
was real.
For twenty years, I waited
at the city gates
for darkness to fall, for stars
to guide my immigrant feet.
Only by dying,
do we learn the true rhythms
of the heart, by crying
how to laugh from the belly.

ELEGY FOR AN ELDER BROTHER

After your death, Hilary,
I saw you flash by in riding clothes,
a whip singing in the air,
boots catching the fire of the sun.
Hunting? for what?
No quarry, no guns, no dogs,
only cloud and rain about your ears,

and then I remembered,
I knew: the way
you held your eyes to heaven,
ran your thin black fingers
over your scientific head
as the runnels of the heart
smoked and clogged,
and you muttering the tried mantarams
of your life: Deus, Deus,
O Mother of God,
Thomas, my Doctor Angelicus,
Augustine, Merton, Teilhard,
my wounded country, my Decima,
my dear ones.

Be still O Hound of Heaven,
the helminthologist, the philosopher,
is dead!
The worm, he always said, belongs to God,
is God,
his sweet obsession, his PhD piece
of candy, his metaphor for the good earth,
his perfect passport
to the Academy of Academies.

3

HOW I SMUGGLED GOD INTO
MY HOME ONE WINTER'S NIGHT

Of course, God can never be abducted.
No way would HE involuntarily leave
his heavenly mansion,
seraphim and cherubim,
beloved disciples, saints and cronies
and move into my modest bungalow
at 166 MacGregor Cres, Waterloo ?

So, believe it, God was into this scam
from the very beginning.
Wife, kids, neighbours, the mailman,
the paper boy, were to move and breathe
and have their being in blissful ignorance.
So long as I kept my mouth shut,
I was sure God would never spill the beans.

We tried the most proven modus operandi
in the business -- disguise.
A knock on the door and the farmer from Drayton
walks in with his wife (secretly invited)
Reaching for the inside pocket of his leather jacket,
he comes up with a whimpering little lump
of golden brown hair, with ears drooping like ear-
rings,
black-olive eyes flashing his father's
prize-winning pedigree.

So, into our lives,
the warm spaces of home,
into nooks and corners,
he loiters, romps about on his short thick legs,
for ever sniffing
the shapes of our human artifacts,

and all the while
oozing innocence   unconditional love   loyalty
and mischief
in nothing more than a wet nudging nose,
and a wagging tail.

Again, the Hour of the Unexpected !
when one February winter's night
the Divine took flesh once more
to show us how to love
and be loved.

Kundera, my friend, you once said that
dogs were never expelled from Paradise.
If you must know, I have one here,
who voluntarily left Paradise for the sake of love.

SPARKY

Morning's soft light slivers through
the room's vertical blinds,

takes in SPARKY and me on the sofa
listening to Nat King Cole's *Mona Lisa*.

His hairy belly cradled under my right arm,
his bum comfy on the braided pillow,

small brown paws hugging
the sofa's padded arm like a lover.

And I'm thinking
of a dachsund's *rabbit* hunt for love,

his master
the easy and gentle quarry,

thinking of music ,the savage beast,
the synchronous heartbeat of living things.

What if the stereo bashed the speakers
with Glen Miller and Gene Krupa on the drums ?

Would the silence hold,
the embracing mood crumble like an old cookie ?

When would the journey end,
how strong are these bonded listeners ?

Beethoven's Fifth, Ravel's Bolero,
List on the keys, James Brown cracking his throat,
and we are still on the sofa
throbbing to our heartbeats strong as *Kandyan*
drums.

THE BONE-THROWER

My dog Sheba whimpers,
and I throw her a bone.
She hungers, salivating
for just one single life
from my cat's heap of lives,
so I throw her a bone.
She chases my command
spinning on a ball, retrieves it,
and I throw her a bone.
She brings in her new lover,
a pariah named Bonzo,
and I throw two bones.
She catches Angie
smudging my face with her wet nose,
and immediately collects Persian blood
in her hot eyes,
so I quickly throw her a bone.
Sometimes, I throw her a bone
for no reason at all.
She is now almost convinced
that all the other bones carried
at least some small arguments of love.

I have now become an expert bone-thrower,
practising my art on the world:
knowing how and when
to throw a bone
with my dark eyes,
the serapina chords in my throat,
the small muscles that smile
round my perfect mouth.

NELLIE AND THE DISENCHANTED CHILD

Pedigree: barnyard,
result of her father's macho roamings:
grey tiger-striped, eyes
from green leaves. "Nellie",

a name baptized with the torments
of fingers four-year-old.
He to command the "Voltron" power,
she, to listen with her eyes, cow down,
or run under the couch.

Before love, the encounter;
hurricane words,
chasing feet, the karate mode,
before the final clout. Animals

testing boundaries, design
of games, the relative might
in claws and knuckles,
feet and paws, the escape artist
finding new kingdoms
in dark corners, backyard trees.

As for love,
he offers a kingdom of treats,
rice and sardines; his small fingers
following the liquid fur
from head to neck ,
the sweet purr signing a truce:
love, before the next mischief.

APOLLO, THE MYNAH-BIRD, WHO WANTED TO BE A POET

All's well with Apollo,
  except for his limited vocabulary.
He distrusts
  'LOVE' in word or deed,
refuses
  to echo the loving sound
in his throat.
  But swear, and he'll embrace the word
like an impatient lover.

The sun-room's summer light,
  gourmet dinners
of live worms, golden millet,
  dead moths
harvested from under the porch light,
  have fashioned a patch
of Sri Lankan sun,
  a native backyard
in his brass-wire cage.

I say 'LOVE'
  (trying the benefits of teaching
and learning by rote)
  but Apollo immediately falls
into a midnight silence;

I repeat : say 'LOVE' ,

over and over again
  like some Buddhist *Seth Kavi* ,
but he would shake the sheen
  of his black regal head, circle
the room with his beady eyes
  as if under siege.

'DAMN', I swear

(thinking of all those other dumb birds
in my life)
  and Apollo immediately squawks:
'DAMN'!
He now cries 'DAMN' ,
  whenever I enter or leave his presence.
Trying some reverse psychology,
  I slowly and softly say: 'DAMN',
offering him some live worms
  to ease his adamant mind —
but he shouts back: 'DAMN GOOD',
  with an air of poetic impertinence.

I try the good word again,
look deep into his urgent eyes
and say: 'LOVE' — —
  Quickly, as if from over the hedge
from our drunken neighbour's foul mouth,
  comes: 'FUCK' !
'Nutting Futs', I swear,
to which the bird immediately replies: 'DAMN
GOOD'!.

Last act.

   Venue: the sun-room,
into which I invite a dear friend
   for beer, pizza, and discussion.
But Apollo resents the intrusion,
   squawks incoherently, then settles down,
 bows his thin head and shouts:
   'Hello, hello, hello, DAMN FOOL'!

I've now given up
   on the bird,
still wondering
   about his potential for beat poetry;
My cat, Pompeii, however,
   has a dire alternative:
his old day dream
   of black strewn feathers, splintered beak

BIOGRAPHY OF AN ELUSIVE CAT

Nothing to go on,
date of birth or pedigree,
I write biography
from paw marks,
stray hairs on my shoulder,
a trace of Persian smell
somewhere round my thighs.

She came in unannounced,
from nowhere under stars,
wearing rich furs,
moving like a thin flame,
my eye in vertigo,

unable to settle
whether she flaunts
a blue ash or ash blue,
like water changing its skin
with sun and shadow.

Refuses to be held
in the stance of stone,
turns my eyeball
on her fur thighs
ever moving, flowing
with oil in the joints.

Eludes the embracing fire
in my hands, an art
of sliding like cold cobra
through grass fingers,
allows me only to clutch
and hold her erotic purring.

And yet,
she was always there,
a presence, Persian aura
hung like an amulet
under my loins,

or like a river
holding me down
in her soft bed,
wrapping my legs
with exotic waters,
still escaping, chasing
the deep sea current.

The night she disappeared,
the neighbours said
as soon as the moon
hung its burnished head
on the cadju-pulang tree,
they thought they heard
the thin purring of leaves,
saw a warm shadow
flowing
into the night,
with something like a tail on fire
high in the wind.

FLIGHT OF THE WHITE BUTTERFLY

O Lord ,   why?
Why did you let her go
in immaculate wings   alone
into this last day of summer,
this field
already sniffing
the coming of gusting thieves?

Where only the sun keeps
its red adolescence,
buttercups sway
thinly pale, the lone pussy-willow
droops with age,
and fallen apples ferment
through their gnawed skins.

Where the grass
now curls in ruin,
and the distant elms hold on
to their moods,
silent and sentinel,
as if waiting
for the shame of nakedness.

Into this slipping audience,
you send her dancing,
tiny white ballerina
on a cushion of air,
minute bones all summer-oiled
for magnificent performance,
to contradict
these farewell moods, despair.

To boast
of the delicate lace round her body:
milk wings that riot
among the bleeding sumac;
to kiss the dandelions to blush,
doodle on the sky's absolute blue,
for the sun to catch
her white fire like diamonds.

To dance
her last act
to this tambourine of new wind,
to pirouette, cavort, gypsy
through the sun-flowers,
arch to the dandelions' wine,
then leap again with the magic
of a prima donna's limbs.

O Lord ,   why ?
why when the sun
finally closed its red eyes,
did you let her go   alone
into the dark elms for ever ?
Did you prime her soft wings
to the catechism of a season,

to dance,
to die,
to end
this voluptuous summer ?

4

A DOOR AJAR

Everything is green down here, and the wash
of blue down here, the coral alone white,
twisting its thin arms
round my skin.
Air bubbles, globes that burst
to feed my heaving lungs,
have gossamer blue skins.

But I must come up
for air— leave the lightning sharks
curving in their dance,
their teeth sucking water
after the red ambush of hunger.

Everything is good down here
but we must flail our arms
for the blue kingdom of air,
our heads electric
for the nostalgia of the sun, the photograph,
the pappadam and ice-cream man,
the green land we left
our childhood faces in.

FIELDS OF BAEZA

"I will dream of you
when I see you no more " - Antonio Machado

I seek
        the small cabook house,
flaunting its red-tiled hat in the sun;
        the sandy front-yard   the jambu tree,
the guavas
        ripening in the green light
and you
        walking past the shoe-flower hedge
with your olive face and charcoal head
into this everlasting summer
    as if you owned it,
        as if the distant rabana drums
were singing only to the rhythm
        of your oiled hips.

I see
    the thatched huts
trembling in the sea-wind,
    ' kurumbas' with holes in their heads,
shattered pots   naked children   family rice-
hound
    taking in the sun,
and I wait,   wait
    for twilight's closing hour,
black fishermen hauling in their cataramans,
        salt-whipped bodies,
their desires hot with toddy and wives.

Tomorrow   may be   elephant,

Haputale's veil of mist and tea,
batik sarong and tongs,
      cashew and midriff:
the cadju-girls on the mountain road —
    and remember the paddy-birds
nesting under the dim porch light ?

IN THE IDIOM OF THE SUN

It would have been somewhat different
in green Sri Lanka, where I touched
the sun's fire daily
with my warm fingertips.

I wouldn't have hesitated
to call you a bastard
and for emphasis, might have even
thrown in the four-letter word.

The blood would have shuddered a little
under your dark Aryan skull,
but you would have held my honesty
like a Temple flower in full bloom,
forgiven my unholy idiom.

Here in this white land,
the senses forged to iron silence,
the mind trapped in a snow-boot,
I must hold my black tongue,

the blood has wintered,
and icicles hang like cobwebs
from the roof of my cold mouth.
I can now only spit frozen-eyed
and gently demur.

INFANT FOOTFALLS ON RED CEMENT FLOORS

Having left
        the green land,
mother country —
            what reason or folly
will ever silence
            that wrenching act,
            infant footfalls
            on red cement floors,
restore the omphalos blood
            that sang my green days ?

How argue
        this dark diaspora?
Do I reason,
            damn or exalt?
Let nostalgia
        flirt with hyperbole?
Is there enough love
        to conjure past perfections,
        forget, forgive
        those strident voices,
        the arrhythmia of the wicked heart?

I know. I'll make the coconut tree
            forever straight,
without hint of beldam hunch,
            or midnight beetle   deep
in the pink fruit's throat.

Make a raging moon,
          the fruit-bat's nightly orgy
          though cadju-pulang and mango
          will still be whole and sweet
          as new-born toddy —
Nothing will fester
          under this extravagant sun,
the fruit-fly will not feast.

As for the monsoon rain,
          there'll only be the beautiful slant
          of raindrops,
          cool massage,
          me dancing naked
          under God's own shower-head.
And havocking floods,
          mud huts dissolving like chocolate?
bloated bodies
          riding the dark currents to the sea?

I wouldn't know.

From here,
          this imperfect beautiful land,
new entrances seem
          rational, imperative;
old exits survive, ride
          the sweet inventions of memory.

The green land for ever green.

DISTANT RAIN

Your exotic pot
of WHITE ROSE hibiscus
has never known the Island sun
or monsoon rain.
So memory for you, my son,
is without green history.

Glass and stone
have framed your dark eyes
and all you know
is that land that falls asleep
in soft white pyjamas
with snowflakes to muffle
its heavy breathing.

I guess you can keep on
asking angrily:
Do you have to hang up your story
like a butcher's side of beef?
Why another poem?

Why roll the rock
from the mouth of the tomb?
what's there in shadows, dry bones?

 I raise tired eyes
from the title of a poem
still new, fierce and lamenting:
"The Rain Doesn't Know Me Any More"

To remember, to remember
the rain drops
bigger than my childhood eyes,
those blue fists
fast and liquid as a therapist's.

How the good earth churned
its red dust bowl,
burgeoned to a riot of batik,
and the sky caught the colors below
like a memory.

KAMALA

Kamala, my love,
let's not search
for blood on the North Star,
or the wound of fingers
that dragged Talapath and Seer
from this adolescent sea.

Let's not probe grass
for polished head of cobra,
or count the pink coconuts
strewn with the knife of beetle
in their throats.

Let's not think of nights
when the firefly refused to flame,
or how monsoon rain
grew leopard's jaws
on the blue face of the sea.

True,
home hangs on the fin of a fish
and my life would cling on
to your flat feet
and bare breasts
as you move from corner to corner
dispensing destinies
of hot tea and fried fish.

What if our children
born with the cinnabar of sun
under their tongues, anemones
in their eyes,
spend their waking hours
where the turtle hides its eggs,
come home only to unravel
their sea-weed dreams
under a thatch of leaves?

Disregard
the tales of travellers
that discount our fish-net lives:
how amber jewels
catch fire in Ratnapura's bosom,
or how elephants walk
under a Panamure moon
with ivory big as catamarans.

They wouldn't speak
of cardboard shacks
crumbling in the rain,
or the decaying breath
of Pettah's alleys,
or how sun-burnt beggars
limp with pariah dogs
in search of a breath of rice.

Let's sit here, my love,
by the edge of the sea
and read the horoscopes
of our fishing lives:
    how very like the turbulence
    of the sea's rabana heart,
    and yet
the gentle rise and fall
of its soft blue ribs.

And somewhere
on our cow-dung floor,
don't we have a coral palace
of sun-fish bones,
shell dishes of crab
and sea-weed to bind
our burning limbs?

And when the sun
has blushed itself to sleep
on the curved lap of the horizon,
let's go home
to the rice-pot on the fire,
coconut toddy
and the smell of seer and salt
from the ever-giving sea.

Kamala , my love,
we are the spawn of the sea,
and home is here
under these cracked rafters
and pale thatch of roof.

Beyond
lies a strange land
where we can only wear
a face of alien skin,
and not finding
the fin of fish or salt of sea,
we'll surely die within.

*NOTE: a found poem. From a conversation
between an old fisherman and his wife on a southern beach in Sri Lanka.*

HOMECOMINGS

Tell me
  of that river
that hugs the monsoon rain,
  takes in the fleeing flood
like a prodigal child;
  smooths the boulder's jagged face
that juts along its way;

how it kisses each piece
  of passing driftwood like a blessing;
makes a home for the crocodile's cruising snout,
  primordial jaws,and the minnows
that seek the morning sun like a prayer,
and I'll tell why
  no frown, no fog
  ever stays over the river's laughing face —
  it knows of home, the journey's end,
where from and where to;
  knows that the mothering sea   awaits
with pounding heart
  for its prodigal return..

I've meandered
    this way and that,
from shore to shore, one love
    to another, blue skies to cumulus cloud;
under an umbrella of doting children,
    still going   unafraid   laughing,
the blood fevering like some mischievous child;
    never forgetting the beginning,   knowing
the journey's throbbing walk
    to this igloo of heaven
or that sun-faced island of the elephant
    where I'm always at home,
if not home.

DARK ANTONYMS IN PARADISE

O my beloved country,
I return like the prodigal,
stay for sixty days and sixty nights; return
to warm my arthritic bones,
listen to your heartbeat,
your new song, what media

and the *London Economist* declared
was the new redemption, the prosperity
Hongkong and Singapore style.
How JR, like the great Dutugemunu
builds another brazen palace
by the marshes of Kotte,
and now rests in his silken sarong
and ripened dreams.

Two million rupees
flow daily like milk and honey
to your desert bowls, your people's
sweat in Dubai and Oman,
the hot sands of Arabia;
and a hundred thousand now eat cake
where once they couldn't find
a fistful of rice.

And a man from Attanagala
ends his life
with a gulp of Ecotax;
and so did his wife and two daughters
two months earlier. The coroner
regretted the lack of early
psychiatric treatment.

I've seen the bustle and buzz
of your Free Trade Zone,
the new adventures, American banks,
Japanese technology,
how hundreds of village girls
with money on their morning faces
move briskly to man the spindles, the levers
that make their new-found bread.

And a seventy-year-old man,
distressed over his prolonged illness
from snake bite,
throws himself body and soul
before the Galle Evening Express.

And how your Galle Road highway throbs
to the low hum of the Mercedes,
a hundred Toyota bodies moving
like dragonflies in the sun;
and the trishaws, Izuki buses
in which your brown bodies ride
with the disciplined patience of ants.

And a twelve-year-old student
embraces his sweet grave
with a generous portion of Paraquat
because his mother chided him
for quarrelling with his sister.

Five-star hotels now gleam
in the Sri Lankan sun, tourists
dip their bottoms
in the everlasting blue
of your circling sea, wrap
their pink skins in cottons and silks,
the loud embrace of batik;
and your craft boutiques burst
at their seams with elephant and ivory,
the filigree effusions
of your artistic people.

And another twelve-year-old
chooses an untimely grave
with Endrex,
because his teacher caned him
for forgetting his drawing book.

O my beloved country,
your paradise story goes on and on
with dark antonyms to match.
But take a bow, an encore
and an encore for the warm brilliance
of your new sun.
I pray
for the slum corners of your kingdom,
your soul.

JR: J R Jayawardene, former president of Sri Lanka.
Dutugemunu: a king of Ceylon celebrated as a national hero
Attanagala: a village in central Sri Lanka

5

THE CHATTERBOX LOVER

I love God, truly, though imperfectly.
But I have this trouble with understanding
    God, prayer, his divine silence.
    Praying, I talk, talk, descend
    into this chatterbox mode, work my plain-
tive words
    expecting to hear the Divine voice,
    answer of small signs, miracles.

I hear nothing   nothing but the nothingness
of his silence, or,
is silence the thunder of his love,
the godly 'no' to all my worldly desires?

If I'm not asking
I'm questioning   whining   cussing:

Lord,
    why the incurable stab of pain in my right
knee,
    my sore back, tendinitis throb in my left
arm,
    woman who fled my home for the dark
night?
    My mortgage is killing me,
    taxes up,
    my goddam neighbour, his wild Dober-
mans,
    his overgrown privet fence!

Where I expect answers
    you give me nothing but
    a pitch dark silence,
    unsaid word, meaning what?

Lord,
    I think your description is SILENCE.
    My trouble: that I don't understand
    what I don't hear.

So teach me
    teach me to listen, keep my mouth shut,
    learn that when you say nothing,
    refuse small miracles, divine hints,
    you have already set in motion   currents
    of my next moments, and a
    mothering sea for my journey's end,

THE CRUCIFIXION
SALVADOR DALI [1951]

The Spaniard tries to reduce
all human bosh

to the slanting shape of a cross.
Fashions the Christ's head as a gathering mop,

covers our mad history
with a body perfect in its pain

from the moment we bit into the apple,
each time we sent our small world

rolling on its belly.
Look again. The pure light

behind the tousled head, over
the brooding shoulder blades,

a kind of effulgence,
the necessary fire.

As for the supreme peace below:
the fishermen, their beached boat and nets,

that's the other side
of the bloody equation.

BEYOND THE CRUCIFIXION

Morning stalks
this sleeping room,
circles   breathes heavily
in the deepening light
as if to announce its presence.

Then when coffee and toast are done
it circles again, watching
my every muscle move, hovers
over my morning paper,
how I tie my black shoelaces.

Morning commute —
I sense some other in the car
craning its neck
to take in the CBC morning news.
I don't believe in ghosts
convinced that the world turns
on hefty illusions.

Somebody talked the other day
about guardian angels, their loving duties,
how they silently shadow our lives,
cling on to us like barnacles,
but without so much as a hint of their presence.
I believe in God
so the story smells of the Divine.

Or, consider this:
I think it's this God fellow again,
the Divine Magician, Trickster,
who stole into my bedroom at first light,
was at the breakfast table, the moving car.
Maybe He just cannot help himself,
takes his divine love so seriously,
is restless, concerned
about those staggering on earth like myself.
Maybe he wants to go beyond his Crucifixion,
continue the redemptive act
here and now and for ever.

Or, may be he's watched
the sweet sand-box mischief
of his two-year-olds too long, too long.

Is there holy mischief in Divine surveillance?.

HE WHO TALKS TO THE RAVEN

talks *to God*,
   black-feathered and beaked
with toe nails growing inward,
   a mouth full of caw.
Superb surveyor of the skies,
   postman to history
happening by the second,
   foul-mouthed, he sings
the sweetest song; black-eyed
   he outdoes the morning sun.

He who talks to the raven
   shares parables,
some windows of possibility:
   if the water's at the bottom
of the pitcher,
   throw pebble after pebble
and the level will rise like yeast
   to the top .
If the desert churns your thirst
   know that there's water
breeding in the cactus.

He who talks to the raven
   talks to the bird humming
with ESP in his brain :
   who knows the distant agony
of the goat even as the anaconda
   unhinges its jaws;
the byways of the eagle's ether flight
   before it traps
the rabbit's frozen eyes.

He who talks to the raven
    long enough, learns
how the sweet wood-apple
    disappears in the elephant's mouth,
how to say: *caw   caw   caw*
    when the gongs of hunger
ring like church bells.

How when something lurches,
    is ready to strike,
it can suddenly stride
    into the face of the sun,
keep the rose between his teeth
    and say: *caw   caw   caw* .

This bird is bore
    and diplomat,
will take your gifts
    and demand more, insist
that you understand its importunate ways,
    love it, stroke its velvet wing.

When the raven talks,
    listen:
    it's God
    in ultimate disguise.

LET US NOW

" Let us now
In the embracing love of the Father,
Wish each other
The Peace of Christ " — Pastor Malone of St
Michael's.

So, my brown hand stretches
to greet the old lady standing beside me.

She turns, glares, extends
a thin pale index finger.

I accept this one-fifth brotherhood,
still believing, still refusing to snuff out
the last candle to our darkness.

THE ACCEPTED ONE

For relics
    a black soutane
bronze cross
    lying limp
on breviary
    bloodied
with the martyrdom
    of celibacy

They found
    the cathedral of his cloister
empty
    Pray, my brothers, they cried.

He now walks the earth
    without
surplice and soul
Father Magee opened
    a door
to the old cabook house
    a woman
and no icons
And God
    did not pitch the sun
with dark thoughts.

SMALL MARTYRDOMS

Lord, let me pass
   the sackcloth and ashes, the body
that must be whipped
   for the skin to flower
like a bloody rose.

   Refuse the saffron robe,
the Capuchin cowl,
   those ancient fakirs
who would walk the fire, find God
   in some cold bare mountain cave.

Don't talk to me of martyrdom.
   Not with my low threshold of pain,
the fool in my head, that beldam hunch
   of the coward. Yes. Peter was impressive
in death, squinting at the Gates of heaven
   from his upside-down bravado
on a Roman cross.

   So, settle for less?
Small martyrdoms
   from boredom's ugly progeny,
ordinary chores,
   common and necessary as breathing?

I mean dirty dishes,
   chapped hands, fingers
that would scour the pan's dark belly,
   wade daily through Sunlight foam
like some post-prandial penance.

I'm moved
from wall to wall, arching,
    turning, seeking the dark corners,
the vacuum's roar
    about my ears, an arthritic wince
invading my face.

Come garbage day,
I'm balancing on the icy driveway,
    as the curb   waits
with civilization's broken toys,
    ichor and stink,
the" Blue Box" brimming
    with yesterday's news, Campbell's castaways,
Kellog boxes,
    flat as pancakes.

And when the snow drives down
    like monsoon rain,
listen to the crack of elbow
    as I strain at the snow-blower's starter cord.
No. I'm not smiling
    at the pain in my left clavicle,
the cold wind sneaking through my old parka,
    sputter and smoke   snow-blast
that never fails to find my freezing face

YES, IN OUR FATHER'S HOUSE THERE ARE MANY MANSIONS

Lord, say: Come,
    I have a place for you.
I'd like to hear your voice
    and please, no archangel,
Burning Bush, sudden revelation
    by the broken ankles of a fallen horse.

It's time, Lord, to redeem a promise.
    Your Blessed Mother once assured me
of the Kingdom of Heaven
    if I became a rosary nut !
I did so, and still recall the night
    I heard the wind bawl out,

the apple tree by my window
    convulse in pain,
some hand clamp shut
    the gates of hell,
the night I found my peace on earth.

I'm sure she understood my pain,
    saw my face grow beet dark
as mocking words found their target:
"Here he comes, fat rosary wimp",
    or, "There he goes, Mr Santa Maria Rosary man",

hobo who never knew
    the polished mother-of-pearl,
only cheap coloured glass,
    beads with crooked cross,
all so entangled,
    no fingers could quite unravel
the holy knots.
So, here I come, Lord,
    but before St Peter
stamps my passport,
    may I ask a few mundane favours?
I'd like my room to mirror
    my master bedroom
at 166 Mc Gregor Cres., Waterloo.

A colour TV would be nice
    (preferably a 24-inch)
to look in on Colombo,
    Cosby, Matlock,
keep track of what's happening
    in *The Heat of the Night*.
I almost forgot,
    I'd also like to beg for space
for my kids, my good wife, Anne.
    So could you please increase the accom-
modation
to a small bungalow?

If you don't mind
I was also thinking
of bringing along
my ten books of poetry,
    some copies of the "Elegies" I wrote
    for my dad, my ma,
and my brothers Hilary and Vernon.

I guess, Lord,
    all this might seem
very strange to you,
    but then again
I know something of the Vision of God,
    the metaphysical state,
space without space, time
    with no name, legend or end,
but remember ?
    I'm right now only in the prison
of my own shapes, the heart,
    the eyes still holding on
to thin glass, seeing
    and not seeing

the flesh still breathing,
    heaving, the blood as the river
flowing, and yet
    I await Your call
that Heaven once promised,
    the one concerning
the small blue beads
    of my broken rosary.

Note of thanks

My special thanks to John B. Lee, Leslie Elliot, Andy Stubbs, Chelva Kanaganayakam and all those who supported my work through the years. I am especially grateful to my nephew, Robert Crusz, without whose editorial and liasion help, this anthology would not have been possible. Thanks are also due to my son, Michael, for the cover design, and to my childhood friend and famous Sri Lankan painter, Richard Don Gabriel, for his cover painting. I owe a special debt to my Canadian Publisher, TSAR Publications, for their long support, and their gracious release of copyright for some of these poems, and to Virgil Burnett for his generous support of my work through all these years.

DATE DUE

BRODART, CO.   Cat. No. 23-221-003